GRAHAM NORRIS

Cautionary Tales from Real Estate Investments

Unlock Key Insights from My Journey, Sidestep
Common Mistakes, and Forge Your Own Success in Real
Estate Investing

First edition

This book was professionally typeset on Reedsy.
Find out more at reedsy.com

Contents

1

Introduction

This book is my own personal journey so far in real estate investing. It is full of stories of mistakes and mishaps that could have been avoided and it is my hope that by reading this book it will help you to think before you make the same mistakes as I did and avoid a lot of pain, frustration and setbacks in your real estate investment journey.

I hope this book will inspire you to be a real estate investor and that understanding the mistakes that I've made will bring success to you a lot quicker than I experienced. I would love to hear from you and your journey. Maybe together we can spur one another to ever greater success and achieve a lifetime opportunity that is inspirational to others. Well anyway here's my story.....

It was an exciting day on March 23, 2003. Little did I know my bride had already got a surprise waiting for me when I arrived at our home we were going to be living in for a while. There on the dining room table was a box that contained the course and materials from "Carlton Sheets No Money Down". Now I'm getting ahead of myself. Let me give you a little more background first. So you know my starting point as it were.

I first came to America to meet my future bride right before 9/11 in August 2001. I was here for about a month and I had to return to the UK. Well she, unbeknown to me, followed me back to the UK and we soon got married in the UK and lived for a while there. I had bought us a flat and then a small house. But she never settled in the UK and struggled emotionally with the culture shock and soon decided to go back home to America to be reunited with her family. This was a very difficult time for me to be separated from her and so I accelerated our plans for me to move to America to be with her there.

It certainly took a while for me to get things in order. I had a very nice family home that had four bedrooms and two bathrooms that was fully paid for. I thought rather than sell it I could rent it out for a while to provide some income while I was settling into my new American home. (Selling my home would be an option later on.) I sold my car, that gave me some working capital and all my possessions to make the move easier. I resigned from my 21 year old career working as a Civil Servant which was the burning of the bridges and a no turning back move.

Little did I know just how adventurous that was all going to be. I managed to sell my car on the day before I was scheduled to travel. So I had a nice bit of money in my pocket. So the stage was set for the exciting journey to begin.

So before we dive into the real estate journey just a little more about who I am and what my journey in life has been thus far. I remember many times growing up playing Monopoly by myself with ghost players because I loved the game so much. I loved seeing how it would all turn out and what sets I could acquire with the luck and roll of the dice. I loved the negotiating part of crafting a deal that would be a win-win situation for both players and I almost always won the game playing real players. I often remember thinking as an adult I'm going to play this game with real money.

As an adult I moved house a good number of times and whenever we did it seemed I had a talent for spotting the deal and coming out on top with a good gain. Such as it was, I was 20 years ahead of my peers and ended up owning a family home free and clear with no debt. I had a good career working as a civil servant so all my potential was locked up on the inside and never really had a choice to break free, in England we call it the golden handcuffs. So I was ready to pursue the American dream when I came to America.

So you can see that my real estate dream was fully matured, locked up in my heart and ready to explode once it got a chance and opportunity. I don't think I realized when I was in the UK that I was an entrepreneur and that I had the potential to grow as a person and discover my gifts. Although I had a wonderful career it effectively stifled my dreams and growth potential. I was like a potted plant in too small a container and could grow so much more if I had a bigger pot to live in and the American dream was the pot I needed to grow and flourish.

Well, I think you get the idea of who I was and just so you know I had just turned 40 years old when I first came to America. So the classic mid life crisis had fully kicked in. It was time to reinvent myself and start all over. I was ready!

2

Chapter 1 My First Real Estate Deal

Chicago Apts 5 units bought on 7/29/2003

My bride must have seen how excited I was at the idea of real estate when I saw those infomercials on TV by Carlton Sheets. I probably lit up like a Christmas tree and she secretly planned in her heart to have that box on the dining room table all ready for me. She probably thought that I would not be bold enough to take the risk and buy it. She helped me get over that first hurdle as I was very frugal and very careful when it comes to spending money. I was much more of an investor and I must have voiced or portrayed that most of those infomercials sell you the dream and mostly don't work.

It is delightful thinking about how much she knew about me already and how insightful she was to have already bought the course. She must have got so much delight in seeing my face when I opened the box and saw what it was. I immediately went to work and opened the materials and studied them. From what I remember I did the whole course in just 3 weeks and went through it a second time to make sure I understood it all.

I spent the next couple of months traveling around Knoxville, TN deliberately getting lost and learning the streets and neighborhoods. It was all very different from what I was used to in the UK. As part of the course I remember they had you set goals and targets of daily activity and I was determined to follow the guidelines to a tee. I quickly realized to attain my goals I was going to need a lot of houses and that led me to thinking about multifamily. My goal was to establish a good working monthly income that we could live off.

It must have been a month or two when I saw in the local paper (yes I know it was way back when properties were advertised in newspapers) that I saw this multi unit being advertised. I remember thinking to myself how on earth am I going to be able to buy that. That was far too much money. I didn't really know anyone to help me with that. How was I going to apply what I learned in the course? No money down?

Little did I know that things would work out. I took the first step and called the number. What could I lose by trying, right? Think of it like a dress rehearsal. I thought to myself just one step at a time, go and see it with no preconceived ideas. So that is what I did. I went down to see the property. It was two duplexes and a single house. So five units in total on one lot. I remember seeing the realtor as I drove up and thinking to myself how inferior I felt and such a fraud. How was I going to buy this property?

I shook the realtor's hand and he warned me that the property was occupied but it was in very bad shape and needed a lot of work. I remember thinking to myself 'So good that is what I'm looking for' so I immediately felt that this was going to be a worthwhile visit. You have to understand for investment property we are looking for motivation and stress and a need to sell the property. Well little did I know how much distress was in these properties!

The Realtor already knew what it was like inside and he told me that he was not going in. I remember opening the door and what came out to greet me? This unbelievably powerful odor rushed out to embrace me. I hesitated to step into the home but pushed myself forward. The walls and floors seemed to be moving and they were filled with millions if not billions of cockroaches. The place was a mess full of discarded belongings and trash. As I went through each unit there was more of the same. I wondered to myself could I handle this? How were these units even occupied? How do people even live like this?

I remember going outside and talking with the Realtor and he seemed very open to the idea of creative financing. He said he would ask the seller's if they were willing to finance the property for me. Essentially what this meant is that they would be the bank for me. The Realtor told me that they were probably not going to be willing to do that as they had bad experience in the past with that kind of sale. I was also thinking where do I even get the money to fix these properties up?

It took quite a few phone calls and a few more visits to the property before we got the sellers to realize I was seriously interested in buying the property. With the diligent persistence of the Realtor and the fact that the owners no longer wanted the responsibility of running these properties they finally relented and agreed to do owner financing. The next step was to ask for cash at closing...so the final offer I made was above their asking price. So at closing I would receive cash back to be able to fix and improve the property. Which of course is a great deal for the sellers.

So I finally acquired the property towards the end of July much to my surprise. I was excited and my vision grew of what was possible. So now I had tenants and a property to manage. I remember there being an urgent plumbing problem that I had to solve. We looked up a plumber that seemed reasonable in the price he was charging and found out later that he was way overcharging for what he did. The lesson here is to always get three quotes when you have an improvement or repair that is needed.

I easily spent all the cash I received at closing improving the properties and hardly even scratched the surface. I had my first taste of tenants not paying the rent and looking back I can see why living in those conditions. They were trying me out and seeing what would happen. I quickly learned that you have to be strict when it comes to evicting tenants for non payment. It did not take me long to realize the system was strongly in favor of the tenant and that managing poor tenants was a constant headache.

Tenants would persistently under pay what the rent was and I remember one tenant would not pay at all. Unless I did something about this situation it was going to lead to a horrible loss. I still owed the sellers all this money and I had these bills now and the responsibility of running these units. I went through the eviction process for the first time and still the tenant would not pay or leave. Even after granting me possession it took further expense and time about 2 months before the Sheriff came to kick them out.

The financial pressures I was feeling led me to rethink about the home I had back in the UK. I thought it would be far better if I sold it and could invest the money from the home into my new real estate business here. I was looking for other multifamily opportunities and thought that by expanding and acquiring more real estate it would help with the new obligations I had taken on. I remember the Realtor saying to me be careful about growing too quickly and overextending yourself. The advice was right but I had my goals in my head which prevented me from truly listening and understanding this advice. Looking back it was extremely good advice. Stabilize your properties before buying more.

3

Chapter 2 - Learning to Grow at the right pace

Gallaher View Apts 24 units bought 9/26/2003

I continued to look for other multifamily units, even the very large ones that were 50 or even 100 or 200 units. I learned that acquiring those apart from the money required good experience and history to be taken seriously. In this search I came across a 24 unit that had been built for the Knoxville World Fair in the 1980's. It comprised studio apartments, 1 bedroom and 2 bedroom units and was owned by an elderly gentleman that had been running it for years.

I remember visiting it a good few times and again this seemed to be key to having them take me seriously with this. Again I was representing myself and the Realtor in this case was an experienced agent who dealt mainly with multifamily. She must have taken a liking to me as she helped me find a bank that I could talk to about acquiring this business and getting a loan. So I was introduced to them. Ultimately they did grant me a loan for the purchase.

I had a steep learning curve and the bank did not recognise my credit report as the British system of credit worthiness is different from the American one. I went to work on building a business plan to boost my credibility with the bank and they could understand that I was serious about buying and running this business. I bought a course that helped me in this endeavor and wrote my first business plan. I met with the president of the bank and his associates several times and presented my business plan. This bank was a small local bank and must have been hungry to loan some money that day as I was taken seriously and they gave me the loan.

The sale of my home happened and I had the proceeds now in my American account ready to be deployed into my business. But I knew that I could not sink all this cash right away into my business. So I got a 1st position mortgage with the bank and asked the seller to carry a 2nd position note to help me with the acquisition and he agreed. I put the closing costs down and a small amount to make the deal happen. This was just two months after acquiring my first property on Chicago Ave. Now I had a total of 29 units in my first six months of starting out.

I was elated with this purchase. What I loved most was this was weekly rent and I collected cash every Friday. Knocking on the doors and collecting rents. I was still very inexperienced in getting tenants and the quality of the tenants was very low indeed. Getting security deposits was next to impossible and could never collect much. I was ulta focused on making sure all of the units were occupied. I did manage this for a little

11

while from time to time. It was a constant revolving door with tenants in and out and evicting them for non payment.

When a unit became vacant I would improve the unit with new appliances and carpet and I did spend a lot of money so that I could raise the rents. This strategy worked its charm and once I had owned this for a year and renovated most of the units I had effectively doubled the rents. I then went about getting the building appraised so I could refinance the money out of the building and acquire more multifamily. I successfully did this and collected my biggest check of $221,000 after doing the refinancing. I had more money I could use to purchase more real estate.

The hardest thing for me with money is that I have a tendency to use the money I have impulsively and this was to be my downfall in all of this. I did continue my education in all that I was doing and learned about entities and the importance of asset and liability protection. During this time I had the apartments put into LLC's and had Norrisworld Inc. as a C Corp. I continue to learn from numerous real estate courses.

Cash flow was my biggest challenge and I was constantly struggling to keep positive cash flow. It seemed that as each month went by I was cash flowing negatively and the business was sucking me into a hole. Not that I had done the initial analysis wrong but it was way too tight and did not allow for the very volatile collection of revenue from the tenants. I had spent way too much too fast in renovating the apartments and doing the refinance was an achievement that should have been factored in the bigger picture and into risk mitigation.

Looking back it would have been far wiser for me to stick with these 29 units until I had them all stabilized before adding more. My focus should have been on getting better management of the properties and better quality tenants with stricter vetting and research. Collecting security deposits and the skill of turning down applicants was essential in being successful here. I was too hungry and focused on acquiring as much real estate as I possibly could and led to my biggest mistake of being over leveraged and leading to me losing in the end my whole business.

During this time I even tried using a family member to manage the business and collect the rents. This is a big mistake also you lose sight of what is really happening and as a result control of your business and I was taken advantage of and lost money as a result. One of the ways I lost money was allowing this family member to rent out a unit for free as a way of compensating them for managing the property. This hurt my bottom line and was completely unnecessary.

Another mistake I made owning these apartments was converting a storage unit into a laundry facility. I used the previous plumber from Chicago Ave apartments and he had no idea how to do the plumbing work and I lost money there and had to hire another plumber who got the work done. I had installed 2 washers and 2 dryers that took quarters. Well one day I discovered that one of the tenants had tried to drill into the machines to steal the quarters. So I was of course very upset about this and just added to my dissatisfaction with the low end rental business.

I soon found myself on the eviction path again. Having to go to court nearly every Tuesday to evict a tenant became very tedious and tiresome. Not only that but it was killing my cash flow and I struggled to pay the bills. Some of the cases the court delayed the hearing 30 days or they had free counsel and it would take up to 3 months to have them evicted and loss of rent for all that time.

Probably one of the most serious cases during ownership of this 24 unit was that 2 of the units were a mobile home behind the main building of units. One of the tenants in this mobile turned it into a meth lab and caused another tenant in the main units to have serious health issues. I was sued and had to provide another rental unit at my expense and free rental for several months. It took me a great deal to get that mobile cleaned up professionally and able to be rented again.

It is also unbelievable what some tenants would do. I had one young couple with a toddler and they did not buy diapers for this child. They never washed any clothes and kept getting donated items from nearby churches. Their unit became a storage unit for old dirty clothes and ended up full of human feces. It took me three months to have them evicted and a lot of money to have this unit fixed and cleaned up.

Meanwhile in an effort to help my cash flow I got my real estate license and attempted to help manage other rental units for other real estate investors. I also help buy and sell houses to end buyer home owners. That however is another business and the revenue I generated barely covered this additional business. I still continued to look for more units in an attempt to solve the

14

cash flow problem. My biggest lesson here is you don't expand until you solve the problem with what you got. Otherwise all you are doing is magnifying the mistake.

4

Chapter 3 The power of leverage the good the bad and the ugly

Lindsay Apartments 32 units Bought 06/24/2004

So here I was with a goal of getting to 500 units and without a detailed enough plan to give that plan a realistic chance. The missing ingredient was to make sure that each acquisition was stabilized before expanding the business with more units. Otherwise you are just multiplying the problem with the more units you have. Give yourself time to grow and learn and only multiply what works and get rid of what does not work.

I'm guessing because of my hunger to acquire more multifamily the word was getting out and the sharks smelt the blood in the water and came looking. One day I received a call about an apartment complex that was available. It had 32 units. So of course with my goals running round my head I leaped and said yes I would take a look. Well from the start this was a deal I should have turned down.

The things I did not do that I should have done. This 32 unit complex was old, really old and owned by a tired landlord for over 30 years. He had done next to nothing over the years in keeping this up and looking back the building was on the verge of being condemned by the city. The most major problem with this was the plumbing and was an insurmountable problem for the amount of money he was asking for. But the real kicker here was I did not realize that the contract on this property was being assigned.

Apparently a well known dishonest broker with a reputation that I did not know about had put this building under contract and was looking to wholesale it. At the time I had no idea about assignment of contracts or wholesaling or what that even meant and nobody at the time took the time to explain it to me. So this crook managed to pull the wool over my eyes because I was too eager to buy. He sold me the contract for $100,000 and I still had to buy the 32 unit for the full asking price of $400,000. Can you believe at first he was trying to assign this contract for $250,000 unbelievable even his friend (or was this planned beforehand) said to me you don't need to pay $250,000 for the assignment fee on this contract.

We even went to another bank that was way out of town that he had some sort of relationship with to help me with a loan and at closing all sorts of things went wrong unbeknownst to me. I was expecting $60,000 cash back at closing and that disappeared overnight. The loan officer who I had built great rapport and trust with apologized to me afterwards that he couldn't tell me what was going on. I found out later that the vice president of the bank lost his job as a result of what

17

happened that day. So beware there are crooks in banks as well. You simply cannot take people at their word; you need to verify and protect yourself in all real estate transactions.

So the problems continued and I had not tackled the root causes. I just simply multiplied my losses. I did during this time get a $400,000 credit line to fix up what I called Lindsay Apartments. I started renovating these units as best I could but the plumbing issues were killing the project and I never managed to get them fixed up properly before I lost them.

With this one I remember one of the tenants was a really crazy guy that used tin foil to stop the aliens probing his brain. He would be a constant nuisance and was not shy with reporters and his antics I'm sure to the viewers on television this was amusing. This gave me my first taste of bad publicity about my apartments and gave me a reputation that did not benefit me in the least.

5

Chapter 4 - Renovating a condemned building

Red Bud apartments 30 units bought 04/05/2005

My next acquisition after Lindsay Apartments was the Red Bud apartments, this was condemned property consisting of two buildings in one complex. The crook I mentioned above did actually own these. My bank that loaned me my 1st position mortgage on my 24 unit gave me a credit line of $600,000 to fix these up. The owner of these apartments misled me into thinking that I could pay myself up to 10% of the draw for managing this project, extracting it from the credit line without the bank's knowledge. This later got me into trouble, always be transparent with what you do and tell them your plans. Never hide anything that is a red flag for sure.

I vetted numerous contractors to get this work done and eventually I settled on one company. I had to hire an architect at a big expense and take out a bond, again very expensive to get this all done. Now as I look back at all I was doing the biggest mistake I made was not monitoring a lot more closely what was being done on this project. You can be sure that when the cat's away the mice will play. I am still not sure where my head was during this project. I was busy for sure but I had not nailed down the priority tasks and concentrated on those first. I should have been watching daily what was happening on the job site.

I know I was highly focused on acquiring my next complex, a 12 unit on Dahlia Ave which I will talk about shortly in the next chapter. I really did not need more properties to manage at the time and have more headaches than was necessary.

What went wrong on this project was the pace was just too slow. I had not developed a timeline of what needed to be done and when but I let it just get done at the contractors pace. This was a big mistake. Also there were two buildings. It would have been better to have one building completed first, get it occupied and get cash flowing rather than try and fix it all up at the same time. My mistake was paying myself 10% of the draw as a salary which left the project with not enough money in the end due to a couple of disasters.

Two disasters happened towards the end of this project. Which is very common. First there was a disaster with the weather that caused horrible flooding on one of the buildings causing more damage, cost and mold issues. Then towards the end of the project copper wire was stolen and stripped from the buildings and I had done all my draws. The bank was unwilling to give me any more money and I was unable to complete the project. This would ultimately lead to the collapse of my whole real estate business.

6

Chapter 5 Dealing with Tenants and nuisance Fire Alarm

Dahlia Apartments 12 units Bought 05/25/2005

As referenced in the above chapter I still had my goals in my head and was determined to achieve that. So a friend at church discovered I was looking for apartments and had Dahlia apartments which were 12 units that he wanted to sell. He was willing to sell to me for just a little more than he bought them so I found another bank willing to loan me the money and acquired them.

These units were largely occupied and needed only a little work that needed to be done. So my main focus was on keeping the property full. As I think back because of all that was going on with my cash flow I could not tolerate any tenants not paying their rent. I remember my next biggest mistake with this one and that you should never do. I think I took this action because of all the previous stories of it taking just too long to get the tenants evicted and my loss of revenue which I could not stand as the whole of my business was in danger.

One of the tenants had been asked for the rent and was late. I remember continuing to ask for the rent and being told that I would have it soon. Well if I remember this right something snapped inside of my head around the third time of asking and writing letters. So I rounded up some crew, went into the unit, cleared out all the belongings and put them on the street and changed the locks. I was happy that we got that done without the tenants coming back.

Some weeks later I received a great big thick bundle of paper. I was being served and sued for wrongful eviction. My actions of course caused a great deal of stress and they were rightfully suing me for not following the eviction procedures stated under the law. In the papers they were even going to try and seize my car. That's how mad they were. I had little to no choice at the time simply to ignore this suit and it never came to court. They must have realized that I had nothing to come after.

I had no right to have treated my tenants this way. I let my circumstances cause me to be tempted to take a short cut. That will never work out and will get you into deeper trouble.

One really annoying and expensive feature on these apartments was the fire alarm. It was connected to call the fire service if it went off. All a very good idea. But there was a fault with it and it would go off and I'd have the expense and inconvenience of managing this, the horrible monthly service charge and the expense of false alarms. I'm not convinced that some joker played into this as well. But it ended up destroying any chance

I had of making any profit from owning these apartments.

7

Conclusion

R eal estate is the main way of creating wealth here in America if it is done correctly. However, it is also the quickest way of losing everything including your shirt. So you really need to know what you are doing. So it is very important that you get yourself the best coach and business partners to even have a chance. Build a good network of business partners so you can be ready to go at the next opportunity and have drive, persistence and honesty in all your transactions. The best tip is to make sure you work with the best business partners that are tried and true and honest to a tee that have more experience than you do.

Always be learning, never hesitate to invest in yourself above all. Be careful in your choice of courses. Always see how the course creator is doing himself. Get to the bottom of the matter. This is of paramount importance. If you discover you've made a mistake, ask for a refund. Cut your losses quickly. On the money back always make sure there are no strings attached. If there are strings, that is a red flag.

Well I hope you've enjoyed reading this short book and that you have learned something. That is my goal for writing my story and I've largely shared with you my mistakes and as I look back, if I'd managed to keep all those properties I would have been gloriously successful and have a much better lifestyle than I'm currently living. So be careful, heed the warnings, do not take shortcuts, always be honest, work hard and don't grow too quickly or be impatient. Real estate is the long game and should be a lifelong endeavor.

Please in conclusion write me a five star review on Amazon so this book and story will get out to anyone interested in investing in real estate. I wish you all the best. I would love to network with you and help you on your journey.

Sincerely,

Graham Norris